Farm ANIMALS

by Michèle Dufresne

Pioneer Valley Educational Press, Inc.

Look at the cow.

Look at the horse.

Look at the pig.

Look at the chicken.

Look at the goat.

Look at the sheep.

Look at the llama.

FARM ANIMALS

chicken

cow

goat

horse

llama

pig

sheep